GETTING TO KNOW THE WORLD'S GREATEST ARTISTS

HORACE
PIPPIN

WRITTEN AND ILLUSTRATED BY MIKE VENEZIA

CHILDREN'S PRESS
AN IMPRINT OF SCHOLASTIC INC.
NEW YORK   TORONTO   LONDON   AUCKLAND   SYDNEY
MEXICO CITY   NEW DELHI   HONG KONG
DANBURY, CONNECTICUT

For Bear — the greatest dog ever! (Even if you ate my favorite illustration.)

Cover: *Man on a Bench*, by Horace Pippin. 1946, oil on fabric, 13 x 18 in. Geoffrey Clements/ Collection Mr. Daniel W. Dietrich II/Corbis Images.

Colorist for illustrations: Andrew Day

Library of Congress Cataloging-in-Publication Data

Venezia, Mike.
   Horace Pippin / written and illustrated by Mike Venezia.
      p. cm. — (Getting to know the world's greatest artists)
   ISBN-13: 978-0-531-18527-8 (lib. bdg.) 978-0-531-14758-0 (pbk.)
   ISBN-10: 0-531-18527-3 (lib. bdg.)   0-531-14758-4 (pbk.)
   1. Pippin, Horace, 1888-1946—Juvenile literature. 2. African
American painters—Biography—Juvenile literature. 3. Painters—United
States—Biography—Juvenile literature. I. Title. II. Series.

   ND237.P65V46 2008
   759.13—dc22
   [B]
                          2007016127

1 2 3 4 5 6 7 8 9 10 R 17 16 15 14 13 12 11 10 09 08

Horace Pippin was born on February 22, 1888, in West Chester, Pennsylvania. Horace was a self-taught artist. Even though he never had one art lesson, Horace Pippin is considered to be one of America's greatest artists.

Cabin in the Cotton III, by Horace Pippin. 1944, oil on fabric, 23 x 29 1/4 in. Geoffrey Clements/ Private Collection/Corbis Images.

Horace Pippin had a natural talent for composition and for choosing beautiful colors. Composition is how an artist arranges people, objects, and shapes in a painting. Horace always worked hard on his paintings. In *Cabin in the Cotton*, he painted every tiny individual cotton ball and blade of grass.

Horace carefully applied coat after coat of paint until he was satisfied with the color and look of a scene. A few of Horace's paintings are so thick with layers of paint that they have an almost three-dimensional look.

Christmas Morning, Breakfast, by Horace Pippin. 1945, oil on canvas, 21 x 26 1/4 in. Cincinnati Art Museum/The Edwin and Virginia Irwin Memorial, 1959.47.

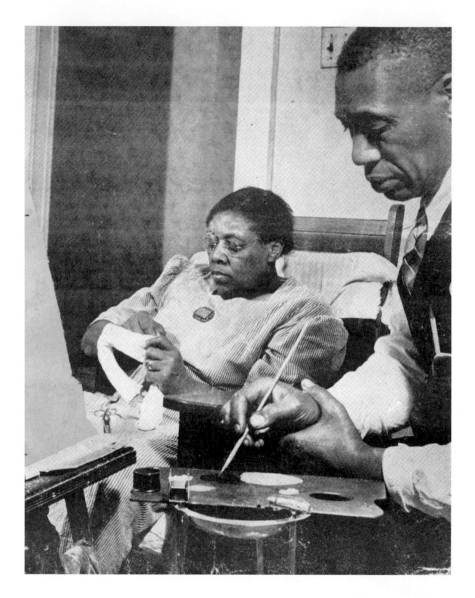

The Artist Paints, His Wife Mends (Horace Pippin and wife), by unknown photographer. Chester County Historical Society, West Chester, PA.

Some of Horace Pippin's paintings took a year or more to complete. It wasn't just that Horace was a careful, thoughtful artist. The arm he painted with was badly damaged. Horace was a soldier during World War I. He was nearly killed in battle when an enemy bullet shattered his shoulder.

From then on, Horace could hardly lift his right arm. The injury caused him a lot of pain for the rest of his life. Horace painted many scenes from his war experiences. It helped him deal with his nightmarish memories of World War I.

Dog Fight Over the Trenches, by Horace Pippin. 1935, oil on canvas, 18 x 33 1/8 in. Hirshhorn Museum and Sculpture Garden, Smithsonian Institution, Gift of Joseph H. Hirshhorn, 1966, photograph by Lee Stalsworth, 66.4071.

Horace always loved to draw. When he was ten years old, he entered a drawing contest and won a set of watercolors, brushes, and a box of crayons. Horace was thrilled. By this time, Horace's family had moved from West Chester, Pennsylvania, to Goshen, New York.

Goshen was a resort town. It had a big hotel and a popular horseracing track. Horace enjoyed making drawings of horses and harness drivers. Horace's drawing days didn't last very long, though. When Horace was fourteen years old, his stepfather suddenly left the family.

Horace had to quit school and get a job to help support his brother, sisters, and mother. He worked on a farm and in a coal yard. He was a used-clothing salesman and a hotel baggage carrier, too. Horace was so busy he just didn't have time for his art.

Horace did hear great stories about the Civil War and Abe Lincoln during this time, though. Hotel workers told Horace stories they had heard from Civil War general and U.S. President Ulysses S. Grant when he was a hotel guest. These tales would later inspire some of Horace's best paintings.

Abe Lincoln, The Great Emancipator, by Horace Pippin. 1942, oil on canvas, 24 x 30 in. The Museum of Modern Art, Gift of Helen Hooker Roelof, 142.1977./Licensed by Scala/Art Resource, NY.

3 Drawings from an illustrated memoir of service in the U.S. Army in France, by Horace Pippin. 1918, graphite, black crayon, and colored pencil on paper, 8 3/8 x 6 3/4 in. Courtesy of the Horace Pippin War Memoirs, Letters and Photographs, 1920-1943 (bulk 1920), in the Archives of American Art, Smithsonian Institution, Washington D.C.

Horace continued working hard at different jobs until 1917, when he joined the army. In 1917, the United States entered World War I. This bloody war had already been raging in Europe for three years. Horace was part of the all African-American 369th Infantry. Even during wartime, there was discrimination in the United States. Black soldiers were kept separate from white soldiers.

Horace and the 369th fought heroically in the battlefields of France. Sometimes they spent months living in cold, muddy trenches while mortar shells exploded around them. It seemed like the only good thing about the experience was that Horace got back to his art. He began to draw pictures and keep notes to help him get through the war.

Shortly before World War I ended in 1918, Horace was shot in the shoulder. It took months for him to recover. After he returned to the United States, he met Jennie Giles, a widowed mother who had a six-year-old son. Horace and Jennie fell in love, and they got married in 1920.

Portrait of My Wife, by Horace Pippin. 1936, oil on canvas, 23 3/4 x 16 3/4 in. Terry Dintenfass, Inc., New York/ Collection of Dr. Harmon and Mrs. Harriet Kelley.

Losing the Way, by Horace Pippin. 1930, oil on a burnt-wood panel, 12 1/16 x 20 5/16 in. State Museum of PA, Pennsylvania Historical and Museum Commission.

Horace moved into Jennie's house, which was in West Chester, Pennsylvania, the same town where Horace had been born. Horace began drawing again to help get his arm in better shape. He started making charcoal drawings on old wooden cigar boxes. Then he began to make burnt wood panels like the one above.

Horace got the idea to do burnt wood panels while sitting in front of his wood-burning stove. Horace took the hot metal poker from the stove and used it to burn a drawing into a section of his dining-room table.

It was very difficult for Horace to do the drawing with his injured arm. When he finally finished, though, he was happy with the result. Horace used parts from other pieces of furniture for his burnt-wood pictures, and sometimes added oil colors.

Maple Sugar Season, by Horace Pippin. 1941, oil on wood, 6 7/16 x 11 15/16 in. Courtesy of the Pennsylvania Academy of the Fine Arts, Philadelphia, Bequest of David J. Grossman in honor of Mr. and Mrs. Charles S. Grossman and Mr. and Mrs. Meyer Speiser, 1979.1.6.

Soon Horace decided to paint his pictures on canvas. First, he had to get paint, brushes, and other painting materials. Horace and Jennie couldn't afford to buy expensive art supplies, so Horace went around town collecting leftover cans of paint and used brushes. He found canvas and other fabric to paint on, and made an easel. Horace said his first painting, *The End of War: Starting Home*, took him three years to complete.

The End of the War: Starting Home, by Horace Pippin. 1930-33, oil on canvas, 26 x 30 1/16 in.
The Philadelphia Museum of Art, Gift of Robert Carlen, 1941/Art Resource, NY.

The End of the War: Starting Home (detail), by Horace Pippin. 1930-33, oil on canvas, 26 x 30 1/16 in.
The Philadelphia Museum of Art, Gift of Robert Carlen, 1941./Art Resource, NY.

20

Horace used more than 100 coats of paint on *The End of War*. He had a hard time getting it just the way he wanted, and didn't stop until he was happy with the way it looked. Horace made little carvings for the frame, too.

Even in his first painting, Horace showed a remarkable talent for choosing colors. His soft, cool blues, greens, and grays perfectly get across the feeling of a battle scene. Horace added little explosions of red in just the right places for an interesting contrast to his calmer colors.

Red was always a special color for Horace.
In many of his paintings, he added red to give
a feeling of warmth or draw attention to an
area of a picture.

Domino Players, by Horace Pippin. 1943, oil on composition board, 12 3/4 x 22 in. The Phillips Collection, Washington, D.C., acquired 1943.

The *Domino Players* is a good example of how Horace used red to give one of his favorite childhood memories a cozy, warm feeling.

After painting for a few years, Horace finally decided to show his work at a local art show. At the show, a famous artist named N. C. Wyeth saw Horace's work. Wyeth was known for the exciting scenes he painted to illustrate adventure stories. He loved Horace Pippin's paintings.

Catriona Leaps from the Ship to the Boat, by N.C. Wyeth. From *David Balfour*, by Robert Louis Stevenson, published in 1893. Mary Evans Picture Library.

Quaker Mother and Child, by Horace Pippin. 1944, oil on canvas, 16 1/8 x 20 1/4 in. Museum of Art, Rhode Island School of Design, Jesse Metcalf Fund, photograph by Erik Gould, 44.094.

Wyeth said he would give anything to be able to think and paint in the simple way that Horace did. With N. C. Wyeth's help and support, Horace Pippin's work was brought to the attention of a successful art dealer and some wealthy art lovers in the area.

Visitors and Paintings at the Barnes Foundation, 1999, photograph.
Bob Krist/Corbis Images.

Apple and Two Lemons, by Pierre Auguste Renoir
(1841–1919), oil on canvas. The Barnes Foundation,
Merion Station, Pennsylvania/Corbis Images.

Albert Barnes was one really wealthy art lover who saw Horace's work. Albert's large mansion was more like an art museum than a home. Albert collected art from all over the world. He thought Horace's paintings were great, and invited Horace to see his collection.

Horace said he never let any other artist influence him. However, he did begin to use brighter colors after seeing some colorful paintings by French Impressionist artist Pierre Auguste Renoir.

The Warped Table, by Horace Pippin. 1940, oil on canvas board, 11 13/16 x 16 in. Courtesy of the Pennsylvania Academy of the Fine Arts, Philadelphia, Bequest of David J. Grossman in honor of Mr. and Mrs. Charles S. Grossman and Mr. and Mrs. Meyer Speiser, 1979.1.1.

By 1945, Horace Pippin's paintings were becoming popular. He had some one-man shows in art museums across the country. Well-known authors and movie stars began buying his paintings, too.

Sadly, even with his success, Horace couldn't seem to find happiness in his life. In *Holy Mountain III*, Horace painted a Bible story in which every creature on Earth is getting along. If you look closely, though, you can see things in the background that still haunted Horace. Near the end of his life, Horace lived to see another horrible war, World War II.

Holy Mountain III, by Horace Pippin. 1945, oil on canvas, 25 x 30 1/4 in. Hirshhorn Museum and Sculpture Garden, Smithsonian Institution, Gift of Joseph H. Hirshhorn, 1966, 66.4069.

There was still prejudice in the United States, too. Nothing seemed to have changed much since Horace was a young man.

Man on a Bench, by Horace Pippin. 1946, oil on fabric, 13 x 18 in. Geoffrey Clements/
Collection Mr. Daniel W. Dietrich II/Corbis Images.

Man on a Bench is Horace Pippin's last painting. Some people think it's a self-portrait. The painting shows a man deep in thought, and maybe a little bit gloomy and sad. This was how Horace felt as he grew older.

This painting isn't all about gloom, though. Horace also showed hope for the man on the bench. Horace surrounded him with beautiful, glowing fall leaves and Horace's famous warm red.

Self-Portrait, by Horace Pippin. 1944, oil on canvas adhered to cardboard, 8 1/2 x 6 1/2 in. 1992, The Metropolitan Museum of Art, Bequest of Jane Kendall Gingrich, 1982, 1982.55.7.

In 1946, shortly after he finished *Man on a Bench*, Horace Pippin died quietly at home in his sleep. By the time he died, Horace was known across the country as a folk artist or primitive artist. These terms are sometimes used to describe artists who are self-taught. Some art experts, however, think Horace Pippin was such an original, one-of-a-kind painter that he shouldn't be put into any category at all.

Works of art in this book can be seen at the following places:

Albright-Knox Art Gallery, Buffalo, NY

The Barnes Foundation, Merion Station, PA

Cincinnati Art Museum, Cincinnati, OH

Hirshhorn Museum, Washington, D.C.

Metropolitan Museum of Art, New York, NY

Museum of Modern Art, New York, NY

Neuberger Museum, Purchase, NY

Pennsylvania Academy of Fine Arts, Philadelphia, PA

Philadelphia Museum of Art, Philadelphia, PA

The Phillips Collection, Washington, D.C.

RISD Museum, Providence, RI

State Museum of Pennsylvania, Harrisburg, PA